ALONE IN THE CITY

By

PAUL KLINGER

Grosvenor House
Publishing Limited

All rights reserved
Copyright © Paul Klinger, 2013

The right of Paul Klinger to be identified as the author of this
work has been asserted by him in accordance with Section 78
of the Copyright, Designs and Patents Act 1988

The book cover picture is copyright to Paul Klinger

This book is published by
Grosvenor House Publishing Ltd
28-30 High Street, Guildford, Surrey, GU1 3EL.
www.grosvenorhousepublishing.co.uk

This book is sold subject to the conditions that it shall not, by way of
trade or otherwise, be lent, resold, hired out or otherwise circulated
without the author's or publisher's prior consent in any form of binding or
cover other than that in which it is published and
without a similar condition including this condition being imposed
on the subsequent purchaser.

A CIP record for this book
is available from the British Library

ISBN 978-1-78148-834-8

*Dedicated to my brother, Ian Martin Klinger,
1949-2007. Not just to his memory,
because he is ever-present.*

INTRODUCTION

In 1985 I was doing a night shift in Milton Keynes, as part of my job as a software engineer employed by the electronics company Marconi. It involved nothing more than "baby-sitting" some equipment running a software program. It was dull, it was boring…and my mind wandered. At that time my nieces were young children and I began to think up a story for them called "Florabel and the Wizard", most of which I've lost and is not reproduced here. It was in rhyming verse, and I set it to music and recorded it on one of those portable cassette recorders we had in those days. It was that which started me writing poetry, and this compilation contains most of the poems I've written since then.

In December 2004 I held an exhibition in the local library in Stanmore, NW London, where I live. Although this was an exhibition of my paintings, I also included my poetry, held in folders attached to the wall! So it was that which gave me the idea of combining poetry and paintings in one book. Looking back at the notes that introduced that exhibition, there were things which I'd forgotten about the origins of some of the poems since that time; such is the march of time and deterioration of memory. So it's useful to reproduce some of those notes here.

I get up in the morning and listen to the news of the latest wars – the first poem was inspired by a visit of President to Bush in London in 2004. The TV pictures of soldiers' coffins being paraded through Wooton Bassett inspired the next poem.

Sometimes you can't do much about the frustrations of life, other than write a poem about them. You wonder about the sincerity of politicians and councillors – it's all there in Chapter 3. Do you wonder what is the point of going on holiday? – Chapter 5. You try to get to grips with modern technology - Chapter 11. And so on… I've tried to include it all in this compilation.

There is one poem which I'd like to dwell on here. In Chapter 17, Philosophical, there is a poem called The Space. In March 2007, my dear brother Ian died prematurely at the age of 57. He had led a life which, for him, was fraught with difficulty, and I'm sure that many times his mind wandered to thoughts of a better place. This poem is about that "better place", although it describes coming back from that place, which unfortunately he did not do. Or perhaps it was fortunate for him, if that place is as good as my poem suggests. But not fortunate for those he left behind.

All of us deal with pain and suffering at some stage of our lives, some unfortunately more than others. Writing about it or painting a picture is therapy – a way of dealing with the things we cannot control.

On a more upbeat theme, Chapter 24, Nonsense Poems, has a poem called Sailing on my Gondola, which is a play on words ending in "a". That's the great thing about poetry – you can have such fun with words. You can also let your imagination run riot, such as in "Wax in My Ear", in which I convert a mundane bodily complaint into a wild leap of fantasy.

I'd like to talk a little about the pictures. I have been painting for thirty years, in my own inimitable, untrained style. I tried to select a picture from my back catalogue for each chapter, but it wasn't always possible and I had to knock up some new ones especially for this book: War, Democracy, Nostalgia and Detritus fall into this category. Others, such as the cover picture (Museum Street in London) were painted years before this book came out. You will also find pictures which are computer generated, without using conventional media. Such pictures are to be found in the following chapters: Loneliness, Changes to the Built Environment, Things I See Around Me and Nonsense. My back catalogue probably consists of about 300 pictures, some of which have been given away, some of which are on canvases or on watercolour paper, and others in tiny notebooks.

I plan to create a website for all of my pictures. When you take a photo of a picture and reproduce it on a website, you can't tell whether the original was on a big canvas or was a tiny notebook sketch. Also, if I receive good feedback from this book, I will go on to write more poetry; but in the meantime I hope the reader will enjoy what is between these covers.

Paul Klinger, October 2013, Stanmore

CONTENTS

1.	War and famine	3
2.	Rich versus Poor	9
3.	Democracy	23
4.	City life	27
5.	Holidays	37
6.	Religion	41
7.	Changes to the Built Environment	45
8.	Work	51
9.	Threat of terrorism	55
10.	The Home	59
11.	Frustrations and Complications of Modern Life	67
12.	Loneliness	77
13.	Failed Lives	83
14.	Appearance	87
15.	Places	91
16.	Detritus	97
17.	Philosophical	101
18.	Things I see around me	107
19.	Nostalgia	119
20.	For Children	127
21.	Spiritual and Romance	139
22.	Nature	145
23.	Animals	159
24.	Nonsense	169
25.	Science Fiction	179

1. WAR AND FAMINE

There is so much bad news in the paper, on the television and internet that you can't help be affected by it. So I've started this compilation of my poetry with things which can touch everyone, even if you're not directly affected.

I have to admit that the President in Town, as well as being influenced by stuff I've read, owes something in its rhythm to W. H. Auden's *Funeral Blues*. Made popular by the film *Four Weddings and a Funeral*, it affected me when I first heard it.

PAUL KLINGER

The President's in Town

Put out the bunting, get out the flag,
Tell the queens to take off their drag.
Sound out the trumpets, roll the drums,
Clear the streets of all the bums -

The President's coming to town.

Show all the lights, light all the lamps
Hide from sight the dirty tramps.
Flood out the beacons from hilltops high
Make sure those dirty rats are sure to die -

The President's coming to town.

He'll see it clean, he'll see it nice.
He'll see it good, but at what price?
Stop the protesters; silence their shouts,
Don't let him hear what they're talking about.

When the President's in town.

The Houses of Parliament, tall Big Ben.
He'll see it once, then go around again.
He'll see red carpets and highly polished floors,
But nobody points out the tramps in shop doors.

The President's in town, his spirits are high,
But on the front line, his soldiers die.
In the name of the President, in the name of the Queen,
They die in their tanks - they were only seventeen.

Wooton Bassett

Long blonde hair
Falling over a black dress
Arms outstretched
In a soft caress

With the tenderness of a lover
Like the care of a nurse
She spreads her arms
Along the metal of a hearse.

As her man is paraded,
Coffin draped with a Union Jack
The people applauded,
But it couldn't bring him back.

His father appears on TV
With a stiff upper lip.
He suppresses a tremble-
A momentary slip.

A Whitehall General praises him
In a building faced with Portland stone.
Whilst on the front line
Bullets pierce flesh and bone.

"Well, he knew the risk
When he joined the recruiting line".
But there are no more jobs
In a factory or a mine.

Governments start wars
To make sure our country survives.
But it's the land they protect,
Not the people's lives.

The blonde in the black dress
Will reflect on her man's fame.
There for eternity, on a
Marble slab with his name.

My Life Versus the World

Why was my paper late?
Sir, there's a crisis in Sudan.
Oh really, how does that relate
To me, I'm a busy man?

This meal is not to my taste.
But Sir, there's a war in Iraq.
Listen buddy, just you make haste
And send the bloody thing back.

This wallpaper isn't straight.
Madam, children starve in Africa.
I wouldn't trust <u>your</u> fate
If you don't correct the Anaglypta.

You said you'd be here by ten.
Madam, there's terrorists at large.
If that's the case, well then
You can damn well lower your charge.

ALONE IN THE CITY

Waiter, my bill is too much!
But Sir, think of the financial crises.
Yes, they're because you have such
Over-inflated prices.

<u>How much</u> for my fuel?
Sir, there's trouble in the Middle East.
I'll tell you what will be cool -
A free car-wash token at least.

War here, conflict there!
Sir/Madam it's the way things are.
By the way, could you sign here
That's for your drinks at the bar.

2. RICH VERSUS POOR

Many times have I walked past big houses and wondered what went on inside, particularly because often they seem so deserted. *The Gothic House,* later on in the Chapter, is the story of what may have gone on in one such house, and is an ode to the cliché that money doesn't always bring happiness.

Eton Avenue

I heard an owl in Eton Avenue
Amongst those Gothic piles.
I wondered if it deliberately flew
To land on the elegant roof tiles.

Had it made a flight
From some dark and misty glade?
Had it been confused in the night,
And had its bearings mislaid?

Then I remembered it wasn't far
From the expanse of Regents Park.
Where it was friends with the nightjar
And communed with the lark.

The cry of the owl so succinct
Amongst the leafy branches
Contrasted with the crystal clink
From the peoples' dinner parties.

So civilised, so chic;
Such a desirable abode.
Those who are at their peak
Live in this exclusive road.

But what about the bird-
Does it know of this?
In discussion has it heard
Of this delightful urban bliss?

But if house prices went foul
In this desirable location,
It won't force the owl
To drop its normal vocation.

All it wants is a tree
And a juicy field-mouse.
Not a two, or a three
Or a four-bedroomed house.

So when the stock market dives
And the crystal gathers dust,
When the people change their lives
Muttering, "Oh well, needs must!".

Our friend the owl will still
Be happy in his tree,
And will make his call so shrill,
From Brixton to Finchley.

Going into town

You emerge from the Tube
Into busy Piccadilly
Where the lights are bright
And the girls so pretty.

Past the glare of the sign
From the Ritz Hotel
Where, if you have a million
The staff won't tell

What you're up to
Or who is on your arm.
If you're rich enough
You'll come to no harm.

But if you're not so rich
Starbucks will do
The staff are polite
And you can use the loo.

You don't have to be rich
To visit the Royal Academy
Or the Royal Institution
To learn about astronomy.

You need no Bentley
To walk around the streets
Looking at the people
Who you never really meet.

You're a free as a Queen or King,
To explore the Town
In your ordinary clothes
No need for a gown.

The only trouble is
When everything's been seen
You get the smelly old train
Instead of a plush limousine.

The Gothic House

The wrought iron gates
Are topped with a crown.
Splashes of gold
Are all around.

A heraldic shield
Adorns the gate –
Rampant lions
Holding aloft a snake.

The entrance is firmly shut,
A camera watches the road.
A keypad requires
A secret code.

Those who know
Enter a carriage drive
Gravel crunches underfoot
As if it were alive.

I passed through the grounds
Laid out with care
A fountain here
A statue there.

Up ahead is the house,
A Gothic delight.
With stained glass windows
Which colour the light.

Parked in the drive
Is a vintage Bentley

PAUL KLINGER

Obviously waiting
For some landed gentry.

On entry I was surrounded
By Doric columns, so Greek.
Ships cannons either side,
Threatening the meek.

Inside the house
Is a marble hall.
With a minstrel's gallery
Welcoming all.

There's an armoured knight
Each side of the stairs.
Are there people inside
To catch you unawares?

Adorning the walls
Are many a noble portrait.
Of very grand men
Who were sometime great.

No sound is heard
In this house so grand,
Everything is quiet
As I reach out a hand.

To hold the banisters
As I ascend the staircase
Not too fast-
Just a leisurely pace.

ALONE IN THE CITY

At the top of the stairs
Is many a room.
And there's an air
Of overall gloom.

But from one such room
Emanates a chink of light.
The door is ajar;
Enter I might.

If I can overcome
The all-pervading stare
Of a portraited grandee
Who watches all who go there.

I tenderly push open
The heavy oak door.
And creep across
The thickly carpeted floor.

At the end of the room
Is a four-poster bed.
Adorned with curtains
Of a deep blood-red.

As I approach
I see bedside tables
On which are lotions and bottles
With different coloured labels.

Lying in the bed is a man
Looking ghostly pale.
He starts to speak
But his voice just fails.

When he does eventually speak
It is in a small thin voice.
He tells of times
When he had a choice.

Of making money
Or leading a family life.
He chose the former
And left at least one wife.

His health has failed
He is at death's door.
As he talks to me
He lives his life once more.

He tells of the squalor
Of some inner city slum,
Where he lived with six siblings
And their hard working mum.

Money was tight
He was working by nine
Sweeping the steps
Of a house so fine.

He said to himself
One day this will be mine.
His dream came true
By the age of twenty-nine.

His mind razor sharp
And wits a plenty
He needed no degree
From any university.

ALONE IN THE CITY

A millionaire by thirty
And girls all the way.
Never a shortage
When they knew he would pay.

Marriages failed
Children taken away
But all with an eye
To judgement day

Waiting for the will
Waiting in the wings
But little do they know
What that day will bring.

He said "I don't know you
Or what you are.
But you have caught
Your lucky star".

Take all my money
And go from here"
Then he died,
His eyes a glassy stare.

I looked back at the house
As I walked down that lane
I thought of his money
And all of his pain.

I had wealth and riches
But one thought remained.
Never, never
Would I be happy again.

Riviera Blues

Sitting on the Promenade des Anglais
In a state of mental decay,
I watch the remains of the day.

A man plays saxophone on the shore
Following some unwritten score:-
I thought I knew it, but I'm not sure.

Not sure of anything these days;
Maybe it's just a phase
Or a middle-age malaise.

Motoring along the Corniche
As if I was nouveau riche,
But knowing this is not my niche.

To live life in the Alpes-Maritimes
You need more than a few centimes
Even in Saint Maxime.

Those girls on the beach
Are topless, but out of reach,
So I carry on eating my peach.

They're everywhere, tres elegant,
But I can just manage "plume de ma tante"
So conversation is non exis*tant*.

Belle epoque, then art deco.
Admiring architecture, sipping merlot.
Looking, searching for Bardot.

I found her, straight from Elle.
We chatted by the baggage carousel.
That was it, nothing to tell.

Monte Carlo Blues

I've got the Monte Carlo blues,
To do with the colour of my shoes.
They don't match my yacht's livery,
And it's causing me a lot of misery.

I've got a problem with my Lear jet-
I can't park it near the Croisette.
I have to leave it over in Nice;
It might as well be in Greece.

I look tres elegante
In my Aston Martin Volante.
But what with the autoroute toll,
It'd be cheaper to take a stroll.

Sometimes if I want to do things proper
I have to use my Bell Helicopter.
Once I start up that rotor
I can reach places I can't with my motor.

I find that when in Juan Les Pins
One has to wear Pierre Cardin.
Those people on the Promenade des Anglais -
They must be wearing C & A.

I frequently asked Prince Rainier
Over to my villa in St. Tropez

But I think Prince Albert is needing
A bit in the way of breeding.

While you listen to the pub bore
I can order girls to my door.
I just communicate with my satellite
To get what I want at night.

You can't get near to my wealth,
Or my bronzed, super-tanned health.
Go on, back to your hovel
And from there you can try to grovel.

But in the next life when you're a King
And don't have to worry about a thing,
If you look under your ornately decorated mat,
You can see me there, I'm the rat.

3. DEMOCRACY

How many times have you doubted the sincerity of politicians and local officials? This poem reflects that, and the tendency now for everything that people in powerful positions do to be questioned by committees.

PAUL KLINGER

The Town Hall

Hallo good sir, could you please
Direct me to the Town Hall.
Today is the day they're making me Mayor
And I'll be in charge of you all.

When I'm in charge you shall not want
For clothes, food or wine.
Unfortunately, the catch is
That everything of yours will be mine.

I'll give you all shiny new cars
That'll make you so very proud.
But petrol will be rationed
And parking not allowed.

You won't have to pay taxes
And houses will be cheap
But, at the end of the day
They won't be yours to keep.

Your kids will be taught
In big airy schools
The buildings will be glamorous
And turn out a load of fools.

It'll be easy to see a doctor
You'll no longer pay for your pills
But all your money will be left to me
So don't bother about your wills.

If you can't remember what you've done,
No problem! Just contact your mayor.

I have it all, we've been watching you
Go here, there and everywhere.

You can't escape, there's nowhere to hide.
Even when you're in your home.
You may think it's as safe as houses
But don't trust that phone.

Look at these lovely shops
Just use your debit card.
But if you buy too much alcohol,
It's on record, it's not hard...

For us to prosecute
You for being disorderly and drunk
Wine for your dinner? I don't care,
You miserable scheming skunk.

If I had my way I'd lock you all up
And cavort with all my girls
We'll party in your homes
And steal your wives' pearls.

So go on vote for me
You may just as well
Because whatever happens
This country's going to hell.

4. CITY LIFE

I've always lived on the outskirts of London, and I love going "into town". But living in a big city has so many contrasting feelings about it; yes, it's so interesting during the day, but what goes on at night? What about the dark side? And what about the people that occupy the city?

PAUL KLINGER

The City

Fountains play and splash,
Sordid neons flash.
You can get anything for cash,
In the city.

Taxis are fast and black,
There's places to get crack.
But watch out for Slasher Jack.
In the city.

There's lovely trees in the park.
Don't go there after dark.
Unless you want a mark.
In the city.

Lots of splendid homes
Have spires and sometimes domes.
But the rabid dogs foam,
In the city.

There's shops of all different sorts,
And many interesting sports.
Some end up in courts-
In the city.

The Royal Palaces glitter,
The song birds twitter.
But there's always dirty litter.
In the city.

The architecture's sublime-
It's from another time

When there was no gun crime.
In the city.

On each single floor
Of the big department store
There's nothing for the poor.
In the city.

If you've got a locket
Hide it from the pickpocket.
You've really got to watch it.
In the city.

There's a museum of antiquity
And an art gallery
And a den of iniquity,
In the city.

The dome of the cathedral
Has something rather spectral
Sinisterly spiritual-
In the city.

You're in your comfort zone-
So many people to 'phone.
But actually, you're alone.
In the city

The Walker

She ambles through the city
Past buildings modern and grand

Past familiar theatres, on whose stage
She would frequently stand

When she was a famous actress
Who performed for all to see.
Every woman envied her
For her radiant beauty.

Time moved on; many years hence
She is old but not frail
So she walks the streets
Every day without fail.

Nobody recognises her
Nobody says hello
She stares straight ahead
Always knowing which way to go.

She ponders on her past
With every step she takes
Thinking about the glories
And the awful mistakes.

Countless lovers and husbands;
Jewellery lace and fur.
She certainly wanted for nothing
Nothing eluded her.

She drank to excess
And often got high
She spent long hours in the sun,
Now her skin is weathered and dry.

ALONE IN THE CITY

When she was at her peak
She had her good-time friends
Partying all the time
Not just at weekends.

On millionaires' yachts
Or sometimes on their jets
The partying never ended
But now she has only her pets.

Her beloved cats and dogs
Know nothing of her past.
But their love is unconditional-
For ever it will last.

She looks at bikinis in the windows
Of the downtown department stores
And remembers sashaying
Along the Rivera shores.

But now her body is hidden
From the sight of women and men
That sylph-like figure
Would never be seen again.

She wanders back to her apartment
High on the tenth floor
She shuts herself off from her past
As she shuts that heavy door.

She turns on the television
To see a film from long ago
She stares at herself on the screen
At a person she doesn't know.

But for a million women watching
It's her they want to be
And for a million men she will always
Be their forbidden fantasy.

Cameras

Cameras in the street
Watching everyone you meet
Cameras in the store
Checking you don't take more
Than your fair share
They're actually everywhere
Nailed to a tree
Making sure you don't pee
Which, if you're a man
You actually can.

At the end of the day
When you leave work with your pay
You might sigh "At last"
But you can't get past
A microphone which hears
Every word you swear.

As you go to get your train
You look up at a window pane
Because you think you saw a girl
Giving a sexy twirl
But the cameras caught your leer
It's recorded right there
On some central database
An image of your face.

There'll be a camera in the bin
Watching what you put in

So next time don't be shy
Give them a wave goodbye.

The Marathon

It's Marathon time again.
Anyone can run,
Running is healthy, running is good
And apparently, it's fun.

Run as fast as you can-
Run away from strife.
Don't hang about,
Run, run for your life!

There's a pantomime horse.
Someone's dressed as a bird.
It doesn't matter whether you come
First or sixty-third.

Run away from taxes,
Run away from work.
Get away from terror,
Wherever it may lurk.

You're on the BBC,
Wave to your mum!
Smile, you don't want her
To see you looking glum.

Run away from the things you hate,
Run away from stress.
Get away from boredom,
It's all such a mess!

Go past The Tower
And up Birdcage Walk.
If you've got any energy left
You can have a little talk.

Run from your religion,
Run from your fear.
You're heading for the finishing line,
Not just going anywhere.

....

But now you're slowing,
You can't catch your breath.
If you're not very careful,
You're sure to catch your death.

You're slowing down;
Someone gives you a shove.
Run towards that new career.
Run towards new love!

Don't forget the cameras,
They're all watching you now.
You can't give this up -
Got to do it somehow.

You know that when you get there
It will be a blessed relief

Run towards your religion.
Run towards your belief.

....

You've made the finish,
Got there in the end.
But what is there left
To stop you going around the bend?

The Marathon may be over
But you're still running away.
Will there ever be a time
When you're happily here to stay?

5. HOLIDAYS

To many people, including myself, going on holiday is an important part of their lives. However, sometimes holidays don't live up to their expectations...............

Holidays

Holidays, wonderful holidays
In a town or by the sea
They're what I work for all year round
They give pleasure, to me

Flying, I hate flying.
The terrorists are waiting to destroy
And even when we think we're safe
They'll come up with some new ploy

Sleeping, I can't sleep
In some stuffy hotel room,
The air conditioning's noisy
And the cars outside zoom

Food, I can't afford it
With the exchange rate and the euro,
I just have to starve
Or go to the exchange bureau

The language, I can't speak it
It's all foreign to me.
I learnt it at school
But they speak so quickly

Holidays, wonderful holidays
In a town or by the sea
It's what I work for all year round
They give pleasure, to me

6. RELIGION

The painting opposite is of the inside of a synagogue during the Jewish New Year, *Rosh Hashana*. Because I am of the Jewish faith, this poem reflects my experience of going to the synagogue. I suspect it's applicable to other religions as well.

PAUL KLINGER

The Morning Service

They are windows into their souls,
So let the coloured light pass
Into the peoples' eyes
Through the beautiful stained glass.

As the choir's note
Reaches a celestial high
Singing so loudly
That the Lord is nigh.

The cantor's voice
Takes an operatic air
And it's hard to suppress
An emotional tear.

The preacher's sermon
To his congregation
Makes them realise
They need an alteration

To their daily lives,
To become more religious
Instead of thinking
Of something more prestigious.

And when they hold
The Scrolls of Law
It doesn't matter
Whether they're rich or poor.

They're near their Creator
And everything's OK.
He doesn't mind
About the tax they didn't pay.

But they have to give money
For their departed's name to be read
If they can't afford it
It will be another instead

The louder they recite
The departed's prayer
The better off they'll be
In that place up there.

And when the choir starts up,
The men can dream
Of an afternoon's football
Watching their favourite team.

7. CHANGES TO THE BUILT ENVIRONMENT

I am profoundly affected by changes in my local area. It seems to me that the desire to build blocks of flats surpasses any humanitarian needs to care for those less fortunate, or indeed for life's everyday conveniences. So that not only are orphanages, convents, hospitals closed down, but so are petrol stations and even public lavatories!

Housing estates are built on flood plains, so that when it rains, rivers overflow because there is no natural drainage for the water. The green belt is being built on. And the first poem has a reference to my place of work being shifted from the site of a grand house in the middle of woods to a distant town, just so a housing estate could be built.

PAUL KLINGER

Countryside

O merry fields of England,
Enjoy your grass in May.
When September comes around,
There, concrete will lay.

Views of distant glades,
Bucolic sights of Arcadia
Will soon be replaced by cranes
Moving in their jerky mania.

Then I'll come back and wander
Past the houses and flats so bland,
thinking of the brilliant minds
That paced this piece of land.

Here were laboratories
Testing things we can't speak about.
Now they're replaced by swings
And a kiddies' roundabout.

They're knocking down the Grove
And ploughing through Pear Tree Wood,
Cutting through the riding stables
Where graceful horses stood.

Look at the old airfield.
There, barrage balloons once rose.
Now, houses crowd together,
Treading on each other's toes.

The old Victorian orphanage
Sheltered many a lonely scamp.

Now a luxury abode
Too good for any old tramp.

The old Gothic convent
In which nuns were once at prayer,
Had cloisters, vaults and a belfry
And bats escaping to the air.

It's re-pointed, fitted out
With garage and a security light.
Neither religious icon nor cross
Is anywhere in sight.

We're getting up a petition-
Please sign it if you care.
This land is yours to keep.
Don't let them dig just here.

But what if I become rich?
Care I what was here before?
As long as I've got views,
And my wife a four-by-four.

The misty distant spires
A most delightful sight
This is mine, not yours,
To keep, it's my right!

The Bunker

A strange building
With doors three-feet thick

Hides a mysterious secret
Clothed in metal and brick.

It stands proud
On an undulating mound
Whose appearance is unnatural
Compared with the trees around.

Listen very closely -
A strange hum can be heard
From machines somewhere deep
In the bowels of the earth.

Floodlights are everywhere
There's an eight-foot barbed wire fence.
The whole atmosphere
Could make you very tense.

There's a bunker
Deep down in the ground.
In many history books
References can be found,

To its role
In the Second World war
And the Cold War that followed
The traumatic years before.

But the RAF
Consolidated its sites
And closed down the Bunker
Almost overnight.

ALONE IN THE CITY

It's all changed
Because it was too much trouble
To get listed status
They're filling the Bunker with rubble.

And building flats
In the nineteenth century Priory
After the obligatory
Pointless public enquiry.

That'll be the end
Of this secret place
That once was the saviour
Of the whole English race.

8. WORK

Isn't there more to life than just work? Some people don't agree.........

The Company Song

Where is John? We need him quick!
"That won't be possible. He's off sick"
Off sick? I don't want to hear that.
Even if he's had a heart attack!

Get the engineer, there's a technical flaw.
He'll solve the problem, I'm sure.
"Last night he passed away, in bed"
What? But the company lives on -it's not dead!

I'm a Company man
I love to plan
For maximum profit, and no loss.
I'm a married man -to the boss.

I need Pete, the goods have come back.
"I'm afraid we've given him the sack.
He told Jane she had a nice face"
No comments allowed, on religion or race!

There's a policy for all, and a procedure.
Tell Jane I want to see her.
The Company will make sure she's alright.
(If I play my cards right I'll be OK tonight).

I'm a Company man
I love to plan
For maximum profit, and no loss.
I'm a married man -to the boss.

ALONE IN THE CITY

Every day I work twenty hours.
I think of work even in my showers.
There's nothing else in my head.
My laptop's with me even in bed.

They think I'm really looking at sex.
But I'm only interested in the Footsie index.
I've been on all the management courses.
I know how to maximise resources.

I'm a Company man
I love to plan
For maximum profit, and no loss.
I'm a married man -to the boss.

The other day I felt a pain.
But I had to get to a meeting in Spain.
I'll be working until I drop.
No doctor will get me to stop.

It's vitally important that the company does thrive.
I'm not interested in nine to five.
On my headstone when I'm laid to rest.
I don't want words- just a picture of my desk.

I'm a Company man
I love to plan
For maximum profit, and no loss.
I'm a married man -to the boss.

9. THREAT OF TERRORISM

It was just after 9/11, and London was jittery. From Hampstead Heath you could see the tall towers of the NatWest Tower and Canary Wharf. I was sitting on Hampstead Heath, probably worrying about all this. And a girl walked by, seemingly without a care in the world............

PAUL KLINGER

The girl with the purple skirt

It was an autumn afternoon
Though not all the leaves had turned.
There were dark clouds and sunny spells,
Summer was not yet spurned.

On the Heath some trees were gold
But most were still green.
The overall impression was
Of a very pleasant scene.

I turned my senses up to full;
I wanted to soak it all in.
The world had turned into a sorry place
But I felt that nature would win.

As I was sitting and enjoying
The sensations of the air,
A glimmer of purple caught my eye
As a girl was passing there.

She appeared quite silently
And quickly breezed past.
Down towards the bottom of the hill,
Down she went so fast.

She wore her sweater carelessly,
Her feet were quite bare.
And when I noticed that her skirt was split
I tried hard not to stare.

ALONE IN THE CITY

Down towards the trees
Down towards the lake.
Down towards London town
Was the journey she would make.

From long fragrant grass
To concrete and fumes.
From squirrels rabbits and birds
To smoke rising in plumes.

But I worried about Bin Laden,
And was concerned about anthrax.
I urged her to stay with me in the long green grass;
Stay with me and relax.

She told me that London was forever,
There would always be the Heath.
There would always be the clear blue sky
With the lush green grass beneath.

10. THE HOME

How cosy do homes look at night, with porch lights shining into the darkness beyond? And inside, everything is neat and tidy, in its place. They look so welcoming, but there could be tension within. Or neighbouring tensions, which estate agents will never tell you about.

PAUL KLINGER

The Windows

It's getting dark,
All the windows are lit.
You can see right in
To where people sit.

In one window there's a cat.
In another some dolls.
One's got bars -
The one with the Rolls.

It all looks so cosy
And very welcoming.
If you rang their door
Would they say - "Come In"?

An Englishman's home is his castle,
Is what is said.
That's probably true,
But you could be misled.

He says to the world:
"While my house lamps shine,
You go to hell;
I'll be fine!"

In his garden are roses
Ivy and shrubs.
You won't find those
In your smelly old pubs.

He's got a hanging basket.
It's a work of art.

And his homely wife
Bakes a mean custard tart.

But what are the feelings
Of those inside.
What inner turmoil
Does that cosiness hide?

Are they arguing
Or having a row.
Is he calling his wife
A nasty old cow?

The trouble could be
That the homely wife
Is slightly fed up
With suburban life.

And all of a sudden
Without any warning
He finds she's not there
One bright sunny morning.

But guess what-
That very same night
She may be gone
But the lamps still shine bright

Estate Agents

Is it the beginning of a new dawn
To see a hundred-foot garden, laid to lawn?

What use are shops and schools
When you're living in the company of fools?

Whether you want a detached,
Or a cottage that's thatched,
Or backing onto a park
So lovely after dark.

Come, see this luxury accommodation
Next to the electricity substation.
Volts, pylons and cables-
But such picturesque gables.

Or this house with its own small-holding.
Forget about the unsightly scaffolding.
There are views to Canary Wharf
But the neighbour's a poisoned dwarf.

It's really deceptively spacious;
There's a garden with borders herbaceous.
But no scrubbing with Domestos
Will take away the nasty asbestos.

A very desirable abode,
There was an asylum down the road.
Now they're in the community
And can murder with immunity.

This is a sought-after location
Next to the borstal and police station.
Those lakes are a conservation area
Although the insects give malaria.

There may be a scope for an extension,
But be under no misapprehension:
The rooms may be well presented
But you could find you're resented.

By neighbours from hell
Who in the night ring your bell
And at three forty-five
Run up and down your drive.

But never mind about all that,
Even if you buy a small flat
You'll change your life for the better
If you just change your postcode letter.

The New Home

The house welcomes its new inhabitants
Without forgetting who it contained before
Their irremovable signature remains
In every cupboard, behind every door.

When they left, they tried
To eradicate their presence
Although moved on to pastures new
They couldn't remove their essence.

When the wallpaper is stripped
The penciled scribbles of the children remain
And the marks on the window
Where they pressed their noses on the pane.

Up in the loft, most items were removed
But occasionally you find a clue
Some old books,
A painting or two

How many feet, carrying what burdens
Caused that floorboard to creak?
How many voices
Have these walls heard speak?

What evidence was burnt
In the fires in that hearth?
What anxiety was created
Hearing footsteps on the path?

What is buried in the garden
If you dug deep enough?
Why is the patio concrete
Just a little too rough?

Those old four walls
Heard laughter and many a cry
The sounds of new born babes
And of those about to die

But the house will keep its secrets
It's only people who can reveal all
The house remains standing
But its people – they may fall.

11. FRUSTRATIONS AND COMPLICATIONS OF MODERN LIFE

As people get older, and technology moves ahead, it is difficult to keep up. I'm speaking mainly about the generation above mine, but I can definitely empathise with some of the frustrations involved with new technology.

These poems are about trying to keep up with the modern world.

PAUL KLINGER

Confused

At seven the alarm went off
I picked it up, saying "Hallo?".
At eight the kettle sang loudly
So I turned down the radio.

At nine the doorbell chimed
So I checked the grandfather clock.
At ten a.m. the cat meowed,
So I took the dog around the block.

At one the mobile rang
So I picked up the landline phone.
At two the baby cried
So I gave the dog a bone.

At three the church bells peeled
To celebrate a marriage.
I thought my train had come
So I tried to find a carriage.

At six the microwave bleeped-
I thought it rather shrill.
Nevertheless I got right up
And turned down the electric grill.

At seven the telephone rang
So I went to answer the door.
When there was nobody there I thought
This has happened before.

ALONE IN THE CITY

At eight a taxi arrived
Just outside my door.
It hooted, so I got my coat
But it was for the man at No. 4.

At nine I switched on the TV
But I pressed the wrong button.
On the radio there was a chef
Talking all about mutton.

At ten a police car passed,
Siren wailing like a banshee.
So I checked the clock on the wall
Making sure I was doing thirty.

At eleven I was tired
I decided it was time for bed.
I fell asleep and started to snore,
Or was it thunder I heard instead?

Remote Control

One for BBC, three for ITV;
but what do I press to help <u>me?</u>
I press the button for text-
what on earth do I do next?

I need to remote control my life;
it's no good leaving it to my wife.
In these days of instant gratification
I need to have an explanation.

There's just so much to remember-
is it January or September?
Living life without any mishap
is like trying to open bubble-wrap

How do I visit my Aunt Sheila?
By Tube I might meet alQueda.
By car I'll get road rage,
if I walk it'll take an age.

If I'm shopping there's a queue.
What am I to do?
A helpful assistant points to Aisle Seven;
nobody there, it's heaven!

But while I'm wondering why it's lonely,
I see the notice: "Baskets only"
I turn to see other shoppers,
looking like they'll call the coppers.

My train goes at nine,
time to join the line.
To get tickets from the machine,
so the inspector knows I'm clean.

Got to remember the zone
or people behind will groan.
Single, return or Travelcard?
It shouldn't really be hard.

I press the button, nothing occurs.-
no bleeps, clicks or whirrs.
So I slink away to a till,
while swallowing my little pill.

ALONE IN THE CITY

There's a man in front with a backpack.
Is it another attack?
Will my life end with a bang and scream,
just the like the worst type of dream?

Home at the end of a hard day,
when the path was blocked every which way.
Frustrations never cease
but at least I'm in one piece.

I turn on the music, louder and louder,
searching for a pill, a bottle or some powder.
Life's a bitch and then you die-
but at least tonight I'm getting high.

The next day I decide my life's a mess-
nothing that can't be sorted by the NHS
So I pick up my telephone,
and get the dialling tone.

At the surgery there's a voice,
telling me I've got a choice.
I need to press one for a prescription,
or two if I've got an addiction.

Three for a doctor, four for a nurse,
five to get rid of a curse.
Six for therapy in order to end
that sense of going around the bend.

My head is spinning, I'm confused,
I don't want to be refused.
Just tell me, is it one two or three-
what do I press to help <u>me?</u>

PAUL KLINGER

How they turned my tree into a phone mast

I went into the garden to hug my tree
And found something strange to me.
There was a tree when I was there last
But it had changed into a phone mast.

I had a lovely pine with cones
But they're no use for mobile phones.
I was told they make a mess
And are no good for SMS.

I looked up hoping to see leaves
Gently blowing in the breeze
There were no leaves, but it was bristling
With things that were used for listening.

There was a thing round and spherical
Made from a plastic chemical.
I was told it was called a radome
But by then I wanted my home.

Where there used to be tree roots
Over which I'd trip in my boots,
Now there were cables thick and brown
Snaking round about and down.

I glanced round my garden
And exclaimed "I beg your pardon!"
Trees, plants and flower
Were replaced by things providing power.

A fruit tree from Vienna
Was replaced by a radio antenna.

ALONE IN THE CITY

Instead of a pleasant emanation
I was baked by microwave radiation.

Buzzing bees searching for nectar
Instead found a radar detector.
So I couldn't get any more honey
But could avoid colliding with a bunny.

A bird landing on the bird table
Would disturb a hidden cable.
It was timed by a clock.
Too long – an electric shock.

A satellite disk up high
Checked on every thieving magpie.
If it insisted with that vocation
It'd be reported in a central location.

My cat got totally confused
Seeing itself on the evening news .
She said "I can't see a tree
With a camera from the BBC"

"Ah" I explained to my mog,
"You see that fallen log?
That thing that looks like a knot,
Is the camera that got you shot."

Apparently my garden is controlled
And regularly patrolled.
It's now a limited access zone.
To enter you have to phone.

A special central number.
And, cool as a cucumber
You give, details from your card,
To ensure that you're not barred.

No more taking the sun
And having lots of fun
In the garden I thought was mine
With the mast instead of the pine.

12. LONELINESS

Maybe this title should be renamed, Alone, as the title of this book suggests. Because that's got far fewer negative connotations than loneliness. We are all alone at some time or the other, but maybe for some people it's more welcome than for others.

The following poem stresses this last point.

PAUL KLINGER

My Imaginary friend

I've got an imaginary friend
Who doesn't really exist.
But while your friends desert you
Mine still persists.

I ask him in the morning
What tie should I wear.
He always advises well
To make me debonair.

When I'm in driving my car
And someone gets in my way,
My friend is the only one
Who hears what I say.

When I'm sitting in meetings
I whisper to my friend
"Doesn't this drivel
Drive you round the bend"?

He never fails to tell me
I'm more handsome than the rest,
Which helps when some girl
Puts it to the test.

He tells me I can do things
That my boss thinks I can't.
He's with me when I'm eating
Alone in a restaurant.

When I'm out walking
In the sunshine and fresh air

ALONE IN THE CITY

We take a mutual pleasure
In everything that's there.

And when I wake up trembling
From a nightmare of some kind
My imaginary friend
Soothes my troubled mind.

He doesn't pass judgement
He doesn't criticise
But to make me feel better
He'll tell some white lies.

When things are really black
He can sometimes disappear.
Then there's nobody
With whom I can share

My inner thoughts
My inner fears
My secrets
Or my tears.

But it's OK
He's never far away.
He comes back again
So that we can play.

If you see me sitting
Staring into space
With the beginning of a smile
Etched on my face,

PAUL KLINGER

It's because I'm laughing
At my friend's clever wit
It's not so much the joke
As the way he tells it.

Remember me when you're all together
Joking, having fun
And I'm all alone
Talking to no-one.

Remember me when,
You're fair-weather friend
Drops you because of that card
You quite forgot to send.

Remember me when your friend
Steals your girlfriend or wife
And I'll still have
My imaginary friend for life.

It's true I can't introduce you
To my imaginary friend
But I'll tell you one thing,
He'll be there at the end.

I've got an imaginary friend
Who doesn't really exist.
But while your friends desert you
Mine still persists.

13. FAILED LIVES

There used to be a local character in the area where I live, who wandered around looking for stuff in wastepaper bins, and taking them home. You may think that that is quite common, except that his home was in a very expensive district, and had been left to rack and ruin. And he wasn't always a tramp.

I'll let the poem tell the rest of the story.

PAUL KLINGER

The Stanmore TRAMP

In every kind of weather
In sunshine and in rain.
He's out searching for bottles
That he could use again.

And when he finds them
He brings them back to store.
He lines them up on the wall
And creates an eyesore.

Nobody seems to mind
The neighbours don't complain.
Even though his antics
Won't make house prices gain.

Because they know what happened.
At some earlier time of life.
Something that upset him
And caused so much strife.

You see, he was a surgeon.
Who was quite respected
He lost a patient, something snapped
His mind was infected

With self-hatred, and disgust
So he couldn't face society
With any sort of trust
Or any sort of propriety.

Then one day I saw a flower
By a tree outside his house.
It had been laid there.
By whom, an ex-spouse?

It was the sole remembrance
To one who life passed by
To the once-eminent surgeon.
Who with angels now flies.

14. APPEARANCE

There's always something out of place. Or if there isn't now, there soon will be. Especially when you're trying to look cool in front of the camera…

PAUL KLINGER

Dapper

I've got crumbs in my beard
And some dinner smeared
All over my shirt -
Maybe I'll skip dessert.

My tie's got stains
That smell of the drains.
I should have washed my hair.
I don't think it's fair.

A button's come free.
Where can it be?
I'm terrible at sewing.
My chest'll be showing.

On my trousers there's some mud
Resulting from some crud.
My new shoes are scuffed.
I'm not very chuffed..

I try to be dapper,
Don't know what's the matter.
Better to give up
And be a mucky pup.

The Camera

You pose for posterity
As you seduce the camera,
Like a celebrity
In the glare of the lights.

With your hand around her shoulder
You are framed by the flowers
Your confidence is bolder
Than it should be by rights.

This is all about your ego
Being captured in a box.
Casanova, Valentino
Is who you need to be.

Your mouth smiles, but your eyes
Give the game away.
Let's hope the camera lies
And doesn't show your misery.

You look forward to seeing the photos,
…………………………..But the camera broke.

15. PLACES

Barcelona, Brighton, Leamington Spa. You can write so much about each place you've been to. Or paint a picture. A picture tells a thousand words, but sometimes only words will do.

Barcelona

There's a tramp sitting
Outside my hotel window,
Presenting a solitary persona.
This is not London - it's Barcelona.

Young people go past
In colours red and blue.
And he's thinking
"What am I to do?"

Crowds of tourists
Watch the moving statues,
All the way down La Rambla.
This is not London - it's Barcelona.

When I get back the tramp's still there
Thinking of his life.
Should he have worked, should he have toiled,
Should he have taken a wife?

There's plenty of shops
And plenty of stalls;
From the restaurants a pleasant aroma.
Yet this is not London - it's Barcelona.

Later on he's gone
To where I do not know.
There's places here as well
Where the raggedy people go.

So how can I tell?
Why is it different?

Only because of Gaudi's Casa Mila,
So it's not London, it's Barcelona.

Brighton Beach

You can watch the powerful waves
Or attend illegal raves
On Brighton Beach

You can sit down on the stones
Listening to mobile phones
On Brighton Beach.

You won't find any secret coves
But you can walk all the way to Hove
On Brighton Beach

You can imagine you were Prince Regent
In some earlier antecedent
On Brighton Beach.

You can wait for Tony Blair
To emerge looking debonair
On Brighton Beach.

You can look for a fish
To serve up as a dish.
On Brighton Beach.

You can sunbathe in the nude
And no-one will think you rude.
On Brighton Beach.

You can ride on the Volks
And wave to all the friendly folks
On Brighton Beach.

You can easily moor your yacht
To show them what a lot you've got,
On Brighton Beach

In the end those nasty stones
Will cut you through to the bones
On Brighton Beach.

Leamington Spa

There's no spa in Leamington Spa
Although I searched wide and far.
I found a river, and a brook
And I found a cocktail bar.

There's plenty of Georgian buildings to see
In fact they're all Regency.
There's a House of Fraser, and a Boots
The Gardens have a hot house, which is free.

Then I saw the River, muddy and brown
Going through the best part of Town
I followed it, hoping to see
Something that wouldn't make me frown

Here's the Town Hall, of many architectural styles
Columns, pediments, stately piles
A stained glass window, a Gothic tower
From the top you could see for miles.

ALONE IN THE CITY

A shopping arcade, all glass and steel
Looking like Crystal Palace, very genteel,
Except for the shops that were inside,
Woolies, Smiths, a common feel.

People, the same, some pretty, some not.
London, Leamington, just the same lot.
Some rich, but mostly not-rich, not-poor.
Shopping, not knowing what they're looking for.

Some flats, all modernist and white.
Nice, bright, would show up at night.
Overlooking the gardens, a very good view
If you're living there you're doing all right.

Ah, Leamington, you've let me down.
There's some Regency in your Town.
I wanted a sip from your Spa
But no spa was to be found.

16. DETRITUS

This has got a category all of its own. I couldn't think where else I'd put it.

PAUL KLINGER

The umbrella lay discarded
Destroyed by the elements, bombarded.
By its owner, highly regarded,
Who it so diligently guarded.

The train ticket lay there, used
By a passenger who had perused
A morning paper's news,
And the editor's right-wing views.

The broken toy is on the floor
Because the child wanted more
Its doting mother will ensure
She provides, even though poor.

The squirrel lay there dead.
The road is its bed.
It only tried to be fed
But met a car instead.

17. PHILOSOPHICAL

Where is that place that people go to when they are day-dreaming? Exactly what are they staring at when they have that fixed gaze – it's something in the distance? Maybe this poem has the answer.

PAUL KLINGER

The Space

Come take my hand
Let me take you to a distant land
A land about which in days of old
Folklore was rich, and stories told.

A place known by Plato, and others too
But not understood by me and you
A place rich with ideas and concepts grand
I need you to learn, and understand.

Let me begin, by asking you
Have you ever seen, in a bus stop or queue
A person staring into space
With an idyllic look upon their face.

You may say, oh it is quite clear,
Their body is present, but their mind elsewhere
They are thinking of what someone said
Or going home to a warm cosy bed.

But I ask you to tell me
Look at their eyes, what do they see?
Why don't they see what is ahead
They're looking at something else instead.

So what, you may ask
Will we find if we take on this task?
We need to find this place where you cannot phone
Where people go when on their own.

If I travelled on this journey with you,
We'd travel past colours of every hue.

ALONE IN THE CITY

We'd hear sounds beautiful and strange
That no musician could possibly arrange.

We'd smell fragrances so exquisite
That will take your pleasures to their limit.
And feel sensations totally new
Feelings completely alien to you.

When we arrived at our destination
At this strange inaccessible nation
What we would find would be personal,
And could be quite emotional

There would be the opposite things
Of everything, to you, unhappiness brings.
There is everything that gives you joy
Like a little child with a new toy.

If a person has given you pain
Here a new relationship can begin again
If there's an experience you have lost
Here you can rediscover it at no cost.

If it's a thing you have mislaid
There it will be clearly displayed.
If you have lost good health
This place will restore you to your previous self.

It's where we go when things are bad.
When life is bleak and we feel so sad.
It gives each person a therapy
When stress is too great and we need new energy.

You go there many times a day
More times than you could possibly say.
You come back refreshed and renewed.
As if you'd eaten fulfilling food

Now you know when you see that look
He or she's on a journey undertook
But it has to be completed very soon
Before the bus arrives or the phone rings a tune.

But that little time is enough
To refresh when times are tough
Like renewing a fire with fresh coal
It refreshes our spirit and renews our soul.

What if

What do you do, when
You've travelled the world, and then
You've read all the poems and books
And rid the world of its crooks?

What do you do, before
You land on that distant shore.
Where your troubles will dissolve into foam,
So much better than home?

What do you do after,
There's no more joy or laughter?
You sit and remember the past,
To make those good times last.

ALONE IN THE CITY

What do you do during,
A crisis that's so enduring?
Do you turn to religion and pray.
Or just wait for another day?

What do you do if
You love someone and have a tiff?
The love that had so much force
Turns into a nasty divorce.

Just realise it's all absurd-
You could be a creature or bird.
You're blessed with thought and free-will
Remember that, and be still.

18. THINGS I SEE AROUND ME

There's quite a variety in this section, from observations on electricity pylons and traffic lights (my engineering background maybe), to what happens when a bus approaches a bus stop – watch everyone get so excited!

PAUL KLINGER

The Electricity Pylon

I stand tall and serene
Over path, concrete and green.
Waiting to provide you with power,
But you only have eyes for the flower.

You never notice me
But without me where would you be?
You'd have no heating or light
To keep you cosy at night.

See my brothers on their countryside march
Standing alongside oaks and the larch.
They're sturdy structures of copper and metal,
But not as romantic as the petal.

So we get forgotten in art.
It's not fair for our part.
We're sexy and here to stay - pylons
Unlike stockings and a woman's nylons.

I stretch my arms out to the wires
Providing current for your fires.
Occasionally I have a chat
With birds who on the wires are sat.

Over shires park and weald.
Over town, city and field.
Over daisy, rose and orchid
Doing my bit for the National Grid.

Listen to my sweet hum.
Walk towards me, come!

Climb up my gleaming tower.
Come up and feel my power.

But don't be surprised at the flash
Which will quickly turn you to ash.
The lights in houses will dim.
A mark of respect: - "We remember him!"

The Pelican Crossing

All the people come to stare
At the little red man shining clear.
They all watch his every move
Hoping that things will soon improve.

In this town that's quite genteel
You have to acquire a certain feel
For who is good and who is bad,
And who is sane and who is mad.

Those different people stand there,
Each with a different hope and fear.
But when the red man turns to green,
They all forget where they've been

And rush across and dive for cover
Trying not to bump into each other;
Just trying to reach the other side
As if they've got something to hide.

That little red man is very loyal.
He waits for the folk as they toil.

He's not alone – he has a mate,
But the trouble is they alternate.

When Red man's there, Green man isn't,
And vice versa, which is sufficient
To ensure that every day and week
They play a game of hide and seek.

There's always a bit of a fight
With their friend the traffic light,
Who's very loyal to the automobile
And ensures it's moving – never still.

When someone pushes the button saying "Wait"
Green man doesn't hesitate.
But Green Traffic Light gets cross,
Saying "Look, who's boss?"

"I've been put here to keep traffic flowing;
I don't want any cars slowing.
You just tell people to wait
Until I'm ready, OK mate?"

But then Mr. Radar Detector intervenes
And detects a gap between
A lorry and a distant van,
So sends a signal to Green man.

Who said: "I've got my way at last;
Now I can let the people past"
So Red man was banished for a while,
And never saw the pretty girl smile.

So please that she could cross,
Not a moment to be lost.
So, delightedly she ran
To see her wonderful little green man.

Waiting for a Bus

Bus stop: a place of shelter and rest
When life puts you to the test.
Away from the hurly-burly,
The next step on life's journey.

You can sit and stare into space
And think about the human race.
Or think about your supper
Or a nice warming cuppa.

Soon somebody else comes to wait.
And it's getting late.
After a while there's a queue,
All with the same intention as you.

There's a woman called Joan,
A kid listening on his earphone.
A girl adjusting her skirt,
Making a man quite alert.

Suddenly there's a hustle
A shifting and a bustle
An air of apprehension
You can feel the tension.

Someone puts a head out
Another has a look out
Searching for a glimpse of red
But alas it's a lorry instead..

The queue sinks back to inaction;
They're bored to distraction,
Dreaming of a film star
Or a pint at the bar.

But then there's a shout
There's almost a rout.
This time they're quite sure.
It's a No. 44!

The bus arrives and they board
Carrying their hoard
From Sainsbury and Tesco.
They've a long way to go.

The bus moves off slowly.
The bus stop looks so lonely.
Devoid of all its people
Like a church without its steeple.

Waiting to work again
To shelter you from the rain.
Waiting in expectation
For the next bus to the station.

The Palm House

I never heard them shout
"Closing time at Five!"
I was too transfixed
By the plants which seemed alive.

But then I heard an ominous clunk
Of a big key in the door.
They didn't hear me shout
As I raced across the floor.

It was too late
I was trapped in here for the night.
I might as well accept it
And give up the fight.

So I sat amongst the orchids
Not knowing what to do.
But the fragrance of the flowers
Gave me energy anew.

I wandered through the Palm House
Into the tropical zone.
With so many different species
I didn't feel so alone.

After a while I felt hungry
So I fed from the banana tree.
The fruit wasn't quite ripe
But it was good enough for me.

PAUL KLINGER

Suddenly there was a noise-
A whooshing sound was heard
It wasn't like a human,
An animal, or bird.

Whatever it was hit me
I felt liquid on my face.
Had I been stabbed
In this God-forsaken place?

But then I realised it was water
From the humidifying gear.
Designed to increase the humidity
In the warm dry air.

I had to rest, to sit
Because I had had a shock.
I thought I was resting
On a solid piece of rock.

Until I felt a dozen stings
Entering my backside.
I'd sat upon a cactus
That had looked comfortable and wide.

No problem! Here was an aloe vera
A plant with soothing leaves
Rubbing it in was pleasant,
And didn't fail to please.

I fell asleep
Dreaming I was in the tropics

ALONE IN THE CITY

I dreamt of birds and monkeys
And many other topics.

I awoke early
Surrounded by the sound of a bird
With the sweetest dawn chorus
That I had ever heard.

I thought I was in paradise,
It was warm and bright.
There were beautiful trees and flowers
And it felt just so right.

I hid from the wardens
When they opened the door.
And at ten to five p.m.
I was back for more.

To spend another night
In that tropical place
Was an experience
I definitely could face.

So when I heard them shout
And I heard the key in the door
I didn't rush
All across the floor.

I settled right down
With my friends who were so green
Knowing that I was in
The calmest place I'd been.

Architecture

Andrea Palladio
Liked his portico.
It was so passionately Ionic
It could make him Byronic.

If you like some Rococo
Don't go to Acapulco.
Try York, where Vanbrugh was empowered
To put some in Castle Howard.

Christopher Wren was a talented bloke.
He started off looking through a telescope.
But he decided to build St Paul's with its dome;
It was better than staying at home.

Pointed arches and a pinnacle
Can make you wax quite lyrical.
If you like your Gothic perpendiculars
Kensington has some nice particulars.

Goldfinger reminds one of Bond,
But in Hampstead there's a house near the pond.
Erno designed it to be open plan;
Le Corbusier said : "That's my man!".

Continuing the Gothic theme,
The Palace of Westminster's a dream.
Barry did the outside, Pugin the interior.
The whole thing is quite superior.

ALONE IN THE CITY

If you like to see wood carvings,
Grinling Gibbons' cost more than a farthing.
He carved whole scenes in wood -
I certainly wish that I could.

If you had your house built by Edwin Lutyens
You probably said: "Include my escutcheons
But if anyone writes his epitaph,
It must surely include the Cenotaph.

Lastly there's the building they call Swiss Rea,
Which you can criticise if you may.
Prince Charles kept it quite simple,
When he said it looks like a thimble.

London is seen in its glory,
If you look up past the first storey.
So next time you're in Regent Street,
Don't use the Tube, use your feet!

19. NOSTALGIA

This section starts with remembering riding on Routemaster buses, but for me, one of the most poignant poems in this section is The River. This is based on stories my mother has told me of her being brought up in Fairclough Street, in London's East End, near to London Docks, which were there before the name of the area was changed more poetically to Docklands.

It's still a commercial district, but the nature of the commerce has changed. Now, with electronic trading, it is not necessary to barter with physical goods; exotic products from far-flung lands. There are no more fog-horns from ships plying their way through the London smog and, thank-god, no burning buildings from the Blitz. But there is a reference to more modern terrors.

PAUL KLINGER

The Routemaster Bus

Here comes my bus, so red , so tall
Or so it seemed, when I was small
It had a friendly face, with colours so bright
With all its windows lit up by night.

The driver sat in a separate compartment
Collecting fares was not his department.
When darkness fell he put down a blind
So he wouldn't be distracted by light from behind.

He was perched up much higher than us
He was Lord and Master of his London bus
He knew where to go and what he should do
Nothing stopped the bus getting through.

There was a long green rope attached to the ceiling,
You could pull it with a good deal of feeling
But all it did was make a little tink
Which always made the clippie give a wink.

There was a platform at rear, open to the air
You could run for the bus and jump up there.
There was a pole you could grab, designed for the purpose.
Especially useful going round Piccadilly Circus.

If you were daring you could go upstairs
Where the naughty boys avoided their fares.
With a mirror halfway you could tell who's alighting
And stay downstairs to avoid any fighting.

The top front seats were really a treat
When the bus was in Regent Street.
Like a magic carpet ride through the air
And all for a one and sixpenny fare.

On the Routemaster bus I had no concern
About where life would lead or where I should turn.
The Driver was my hero, the Clippie my Queen
Protecting little me, sitting between.

The River

They told me to go down to the river
To watch the water flow.
They said the river is soothing,
And will make your troubles go.

I went down to the river
To search for my distant past,
But all I saw was buildings:
Giant blocks of glass.

Where were the docks and cranes?
Where were the smells of spice?
Where were the magical goods
From some far-off paradise?

It's all coming back to me now-
Ships' foghorns through the smog.
The lap of the water against
The banks, or some floating logs.

PAUL KLINGER

I wandered through the streets;
Strange accents I could hear.
Talk of money and finance,
Or the price of the latest share.

No talk of distant lands,
Or of seas rough and high.
No smells of oily cranes
Or a cheery docker's cry.

I want to live by the river,
But I'm not a billionaire.
That's what you need to be
If you want to live just here.

I stared into the water
To see what I might find-
Swirling masses of blackness,
Patterns of all different kinds.

The water cleared and I could see
The past as clear as day.
I could see flames and hear the planes-
An awesome, terrible affray.

London survived the Blitz,
And she will survive the new terror.
Let no-one forget that fact,
Let nobody make that error.

My life is like the river -
It is changing all the time.
Flowing, ebbing, swirling,
Aquatic, maritime.

So come, see the river.
Watch the water flow.
Look - the river is soothing,
It'll make your troubles go,

Life As it was

Can you imagine life
Without the internet?
When the only surfing you could do
Involved getting very wet?

Can you imagine a phone
Attached to the wall?
When you'd speak through a wire
Which would relay your call

When there were only two channels
On the television
And what to watch
Was an easy decision.

You could drive into town
Without a congestion charge,
And the parking meter fee
Wasn't really too large.

Emails weren't around,
You couldn't send a text
And instead of a fax
Was a thing called telex.

If you wanted to travel
In your car from A to B
You'd use a paper map
But now that's history.

There was no satellite navigation
Nor Google Earth
Which nowadays can take you
From London to Perth

There were no Blackberries
There were no laptops
And Windows were things
Which were in front of shops.

But instead, in your lap
You'd hold a solid tome
In front of the fire
And you were really home.

What happened to those years?

What happened to those years?
Those years up to three.
They were real at the time
But now forgotten by me.

What did I see
When I first opened my eyes
Probably my mother
I would have heard her sighs.

ALONE IN THE CITY

The family that I loved
Cousins, uncles and aunts
Such a fuss of me was made
In cafes and restaurants.

My first time to crawl
My first time to stand
I'm sure I know
Who first gave me her hand.

My first little laugh
My first spoken word
Some strange interpretation
Of something I heard.

Why can't I recall
The funny words I would say.
The clues lie with those now old
But how long will they stay?

Why can't I remember
The sweet clothes I wore
The little peaked hat
That my mother adored?

I see children of my family
Of those sorts of years.
Who seem to have acquired
The same hopes and fears

I want to write it all down
And keep it for them.
But God doesn't want us to know
What we knew then.

20. CHILDREN'S POEMS

The first poem is called the Kalamazoo. Apparently that's the name of a city in America. I didn't know that at first – I thought it was the name of a photocopying machine company. So that's good; hopefully I can't be sued now! I just liked the name. And there's the Ant and the Elephant - it must have been the extremes that inspired me.

PAUL KLINGER

The Kalamazoo

Have you heard of the kalamazoo,
Or of the crazy things it can do?
Well, just listen, I'm telling you
Don't mess with the kalamazoo!

The kalamazoo is a big pink blob.
It likes you best when you call it Bob.
But it doesn't look like a Bob, or a Jack.
It looks like a marshmallow under attack.

It has six legs and five eyes.
It has a particular fondness for French fries.
And if you're unlucky enough to get near,
It'll squeeze you harder than you can bear.

But then it'll pretend to be kind
It'll tell you to relax, unwind.
Just when you're feeling all calm
It'll jump on your tummy and twist your arm.

And twist and twist until you scream
And bribe it with offers of ice cream.
Just as long as it lets you go
And is your friend, not your foe.

It's a crafty devil, that Kalamazoo.
It'll come up behind you and go Boo!
That'll make you laugh, unaware
That it's stolen your apple and your pear.

The kalamazoo has an extra sense.
It knows when you're carrying fifty pence.

Then it gets out its fiddle and plays
So that you reward it for its musical ways.

But then you find you've no money left.
And you go home all bereft.
While the kalamazoo gloats over its hoard
Of pennies you gave it for its reward.

Don't go near it when the moon is full.
Strange things happen - quite awful.
The kalamazoo suddenly turns green
And looks for a child under thirteen.

And when it finds a suitable kid
It pops it into a pot, and closes the lid.
And if that child doesn't escape,
It comes out a very funny shape.

Ready for the Kalamazoo's supper
To be eaten with bread and butter
And perhaps a brandy snap.
Then it goes to take a nap.

But if you want to beat the Kalamazoo
I'll tell you what you must do.
Creep up behind it and shout "Shlikitishik!"
Whilst poking it with a celery stick.

And whilst its defences are down
And you see it's beginning to frown,
Hit it with some rotten broccoli;
It'll make it go all wobbly.

It'll start to talk gobblygook
And shout "I think I'm going to zook!"
Then break into little bits.
It'll frighten you out of your wits!

It's actually quite sad
Because it wasn't always so bad.
That'll be the end of the kalamazoo,
Unless you've got some glue.

The Castle Door

Behold, the castle door, so strong so high
What secrets lie within?
No sound escapes, of habitation inside
Except the howling of the winter wind.

Turreted walls, a moat so deep
A drawbridge that can be raised
What do you shield, oh house of strength?
Possibly a distressed maid?

Or possibly a wizard, with long white beard
And a cape decorated with stars and moon.
Or a witch, stirring a cauldron
Humming a sinister tune.

We know not what happens inside.
Is metal turned to gold?
In such a place alchemy was rife
If we believe what we are told.

ALONE IN THE CITY

I watched the place from the nearby wood
Until day turned to night
At midnight there came a ghostly sound
I was rewarded with an amazing sight.

The drawbridge was lowered
But I could see no sight of man.
Suddenly a white horse appeared.
It galloped across the moonlit land.

Followed by an owl, its hoot like a cry
It came from the castle roof
Al I could hear was its sound
And the sound of galloping hoof.

Then suddenly a wind picked up
So strong it was, like a gale
Whistling through the barren trees
Making a cry and a wail.

Things were flying in my face
I knew not what they were
I started to run, to get out of this place
To somewhere much safer.

I turned to take a final look
At the castle, over my shoulder
But a mist had come, the temperature had dropped
I felt so much colder.

Years later I returned to the spot
Where the mysterious castle had been.
But in place of the moat was a lake
The water had a curious sheen.

No castle was in that location,
Though I knew I had made not been mistaken.
It was if water had filled in the place
From where the castle was taken.

I often dream of the castle and moat
In my dreams I hear the galloping horse.
Something was there that night
Some presence, spirit or force.

What was the horse running from?
Why did the owl follow?
But then I forget it, and go back to sleep.
It's another day tomorrow

The Garden Shed

Night-time was here, there was a full moon
Little children were asleep in their beds
Dreaming of toys of all different colours,
Green and blue and red.

But while all the people slept
Their cat was wide awake
Walking up and down the garden
Past the spade and the garden rake..

While slinking down the garden path
The cat heard a noise
Coming from the garden shed
Where Mummy kept the toys

ALONE IN THE CITY

As it got closer the noise grew loud
It was very pleasing to the ear
It was music, that's for sure
A jolly tune to hear.

The cat stretched out a paw,
And yanked the door open wide
What it saw put its fur on end
And its head tilt to one side

There in the shed was a garden band
Made up of animals and birds
The rhythm was good, the beat was cool
You didn't need to hear the words

A fox was on guitar, a dog on drums
A magpie provided the voice
The cat's paws were moving to the beat
There was really no choice

A squirrel played piano
A rabbit played double bass
When that rabbit played a riff
Boy you should have seen its face

All the night time animals
Came down to join in the fun
A hedgehog did a jig
And a snail broke into a run.

Worms came out of the grass
Wriggling to the beat.
A tortoise and a frog
At last got to meet.

But it all came to an end
When mummy suddenly woke.
She opened her window wide
And realised it was no joke.

Worried that her children
Would be woken by the band
She rushed down the garden
It was after all, her land.

She shouted to the animals
I'll give you five minutes to stop
Or if you don't
I'll be sure to call the cops.

So off went the squirrel;
The fox and magpie too.
The dog chased the rabbit out
Thinking it would make a nice stew.

Mummy locked the shed
And picked the cat up in her arms
Together they went back to the house
And everything now was calm.

But if you listened carefully
You could still hear a tune
The animals had found the shed next door
Where there was even more room.

The little children slept on
The moon still shone so bright
And the animals kept playing
Right through the night.

The Ant and The Elephant

An ant with no dependant
Fell in love with an elephant
Because it was important
To have a next of kin.

Although not healthy
The ant was wealthy
From the time when he was stealthy
And hoarded specks of gold.

He had a flat in Cannes
And one in Juan les Pins,
Also a caravan
In which he travelled everywhere.

To see the two courting
Was really rather sporting
And actually quite daunting
Considering the difference in size.

In moments of elation
Without any invitation
The elephant showed to the nation
The ant at the end of his trunk.

They were married at Caxton Hall
Everyone came to the Ball
They honeymooned in Nepal
And returned deeply in love.

The ant added to his will
A special codicil

To pay any large bill
For juicy bamboo shoots.

Alas the story is told
The elephant caught a cold
And with a sneeze ever so bold
She blew the ant away.

He is not seen anymore
But the elephant's quite sure
That her insect brother-in-law
Is really rather cute.

The Slug

There's a slug on the patio
That seems in a fix.
It's surrounded by ants
Who seem to want to mix.

It keeps on wriggling
As if it's in pain.
I ought to do something
Before it starts to rain.

I pick up a leaf
And push it aboard.
I put it on a ledge
Where its safety's assured.

I go inside
To have my lunchtime beer.
When I come back
It's no longer there.

Is it safe,
Should I get involved.
Or has it gone off to die-
Problem solved?

The Sea

From where I stand I can see the sea-
There's a seagull flying straight at me!
I think I'll turn straight around,
And head back up to London Town.

From where I stand I can see the farm-
And a goose that wants to do me harm.
Do you mind if I take this road
To return to my previous abode?

From where I stand I can see the lake-
With a heron that seems to be on the make.
He's standing there very still,
Looking for something nice to kill.

From where I stand I can see the pond-
There's a duck wanting me to respond.
However, never having mastered the quack
I decide it's high time for me to pack.

From where I stand I can see horses loose,
And a very threatening Canada Goose.
So I quickly consult my A to Z
To find my way straight back to bed.

21. SPIRITUAL AND ROMANTIC POEMS

I have chosen the painting opposite because it suggests romance, with the couple holding hands within the portico of a beautiful Greek or Roman temple, and spiritualism, as suggested by the bright colours of the beach-hut-like structures, with possibly something lurking behind the hut windows. Could that something be the spirits of former lovers?

PAUL KLINGER

The Subject of our Love

I present a colour to the world.
You present a different colour, it's true.
When we flow together the colour's fresh and new.
It's the chemistry of love.

I carry on along my own path.
Your path collides with mine.
Together we merge and our energy shines.
It's the physics of love.

I thrive in light that's good and bright
You thrive in the warm and dry.
Together we're an exotic plant growing high.
It's the biology of love.

When I add the words you say to me
To those you said before
The addition reaches a loving score.
It's the mathematics of love.

What you give to me now
Comes from your warm-hearted past.
Where no hate could ever last.
It's the history of love.

If I live where I am now
And you are far away
Our bond is here to stay.
It's the geography of love.

All the scholars of the world
Could study our lives together.

And in any subject, whichever
They'd never understand our love.

The Lake

The moon shines on the silent snow
Showing the night-folk the way to go.
The star sends down its twinkling ray
Helping the fairy on her way.

She gently wakes a sleeping bird
To tell him of the things she's heard.
She passes on a mystery known
To only those who have flown.

The lucky creatures of the air
Have qualities with which we can't compare:
They're nearer to God and they can see
All that goes on between you and me.

I heard a story about a terrible place,
Where the things men did were a disgrace.
The bird folk stopped singing there
Never to come back, 'cept to shed a tear.

So let the birds eat the berry
To keep their little ones all so merry.
They will tell of all you've done
And whisper it to the rays of the sun.

The fairy will go to the lake at night
To prepare her reckoning for first daylight.
If the day's sunny all will be revealed
By the water-sprites that come from the field.

The mysteries of the curious lake,
The lovely patterns the reflections make,
Moving dappled shadows on the tree,
Giving forth signals we cannot see.

Those are signals to our Maker
Whoever is our Creator
Flashing up what the night-folk told,
In jewels of light and rays of gold.

You and I

If I am here and you are there
Do you still think of me?
If I am there and you are here
Does life pass pleasantly?

If I decide to go away
Do you hope I come back quick?
Even though it's here you stay
Do you watch every second tick?

If I am here and you are there
I bet you have a ball.
If I am there and you are here
You think of me not at all!

In fact if I decide to go away,
You say "Don't hurry home"
Even though it's here you stay,
I ring and get the answer-phone.

22. NATURE

This section includes a poem about Fowey, my favourite Cornish village, or some may call it a town. I wrote this in 2002, although it invoked memories of a few years earlier, when what is now flats overlooking the river was actually a hotel, near the Boddinick ferry. Fowey has many connotations: Daphne du Maurier, English China Clay, the Wind in the Willows, to name a few. It inspires poetry.

PAUL KLINGER

Nature

The pauper starves, while the king enjoys his feast,
And the sun rises in the East.

Whether your fate is bad, or with luck your blessed
The sun sets in the West.

Whether we live or whether we die
The clouds blow in the sky.

You can strive to win or give up the fight
But the stars still shine in the night..

Whether the sad refrain or the happy tune
The earth is circled by the moon.

Your life is a drag, or it may be fun
But the earth still goes round the sun.

We may know where we're going or hate where we've been,
The leaves on the tree are green.

Man can live in peace or fight ten wars
But nothing stops Nature's unwritten laws.

Last Night at Fowey

The moonlight plays on the water,
Playing all along the estuary.
My eyes feast on this visual delight;
I feel calm seeping through the rest of me.

ALONE IN THE CITY

The pool of white light cannot rest-
It's constantly invaded,
By little boats with little lights
Changing from green to red unaided.

But then - what is this:-
A giant moving hulk
Moving silently upriver
Carrying clay in bulk.

The tug Pendennick returns,
From escorting the hulk to the sea.
It makes the water swirl
So that its calm was history.

The tug's wake is like a bride's train
With bits of black and white.
But this tug is no virgin-
It's a lady of the night.

I continue to watch the light
And I can gradually discern
A string of yachts moored
Patiently waiting their turn.

As they wait they listen
To the cries of the gulls and birds.
To us it sounds like squabbles
But they understand all the words.

The yachts and gulls understand
The strange life of the ocean.
If we don't go to sea, to us,
It's a completely different notion.

Gradually the moon shifts
I can't see the yachts so clearly.
The spire in Place House chimes eleven;
It's time for bed, nearly.

And through the long night
If I cannot sleep,
Across the room I will creep
To watch the water so deep.

There's no more little boats
No lights of green and red.
Now the water can play
And shimmer in white instead.

The music of the ripples
Plays its own sweet tune
It sings through the night
Come back boats, come back soon!.

Eyes II

Look into my eyes,
Look into my eyes.
Windows into my soul,
Is that where my secret lies?

Listen to my voice.
Listen to my voice.
Hear what I say,
Then make your choice.

Read my mind.
Read my mind.
Come to your conclusions
About what you find.

Feel my emotion.
Feel my emotion.
Will you turn away,
Or give me your devotion?

My eyes are clear,
My voice is low.
What my mind has there
My emotions will show.

Look into my eyes.
Look into my eyes.
Windows into my soul,
There, no secret lies.

Enigma Wood 2

Enigma Wood
If you could,
Would you reveal
Your strange appeal?

The bird song is sweet
And everyone I met
Has a smile
All the while.

The sun dapples through
In glades anew
With bright tall flowers
Standing like towers.

But when I leave
I cannot perceive
The same good feeling
I can feel it leaving

As I step into the road
I can feel the load
Come back to my mind
As the lane winds.

After 7/7

Daisy, big daisy, tall daisy,
The wind moves you , sways you.
You talk to me, whispering
Your message of explanation, reassuring.

I wish I could understand
But I know that every turn, and twist,
And bow, and dip, so gentle
Represents a message, elemental.

I cannot understand now
What it is you are saying
But those poor dear souls blown away-
They now understand your sway.

ALONE IN THE CITY

What happened yesterday
To London Town, Dear London
Our London Town, Your London Town
Bombs won't bring our gardens down.

You nod to me, your gentle petals
Pointing in all directions, and yet
Perfectly in harmony and calm
I want to hold you in my palm.

And look and feel and smell
Your goodness, your simple life
That God created in our garden.
I pray that He won't pardon

Those who destroy and take away
His creatures, whatever/whoever.
The destroyers are not of his kind,
They have no heart, soul or mind.

Those who've gone will understand the flower
The bird, the bee, the bush,
The moon, the sun, the sea
And will rest in peace for eternity.

The Oak Tree

From horse and cart
To aeroplanes in the sky
Every type of vehicle
Has passed me by.

PAUL KLINGER

I've seen people change
Over many passing year
With different colour skin
With different things to wear.

From Elizabethan dress
To the burka and veil
People brown and tanned
And some very pale.

People have sheltered
Under me in the rain.
And lovers, in the sunshine
Next to me have lain.

I've seen highwaymen demand
"Your money or your life".
And muggers with hoods
Threatening with a knife.

I was once part of the grounds
Of a vast stately home,
Which is now a park
Where anyone can roam.

Although buildings appear
I have always remained
Protected by the monarch
Whoever it was that reigned.

When Henry the Eighth decided
To end the monasteries,
He sold the land
But kept the trees.

ALONE IN THE CITY

When King George employed
The gardener Capability Brown
The aristocracy came
To the country from the town.

So I just kept growing,
Getting bigger in the girth.
So much bigger than
The twig I was at birth.

When springtime comes
My branches are full of nests.
All my feathered friends
Come to me to rest.

I have so many friends
Among the creatures of the air,
They fly by day,
At night they come back here.

Pigeons, jays, sparrows,
Robins and crow.
I know all their names,
And where they go.

Children are my friends
They climb up in my leaves of green
And in the hole in my trunk
They don't tell what they've seen

It's no good telling adults
About a fairy or an elf
They might as well
Keep it to their self.

I've been around so long
Since the sixteenth century
I could tell many a tale
And many a good story.

I didn't have a phone
Way back then
But I picked up gossip
From passing men.

Experts want to interrogate
To find out about history
But they'll get nowhere
Because this is just poetry.

This Green and pleasant Land

A gentle breeze blows through the grass
Waving like a choppy sea
Whilst hurricanes rage through Pacific lands
Causing havoc and tragedy.

The wind in the trees causes a rustle and a stir
The sound is a symphony.
Whilst volcanoes rock some parts of Japan
So terribly violently.

The garden plants shake in a gentle way
Nodding to you and me,
As avalanches hit the Alps
Bringing down rocks and scree.

The water in the garden pond
Ripples and catches the sun
As Africa suffers from enduring drought
Providing water for no-one.

The geraniums look radiant
In their dress of green and red
Whilst paddy fields in India
Flood and leave cattle dead.

The six-o-clock news tells of English floods,
A village in Cornwall is destroyed.
So God doesn't forget England
When with us he's annoyed.

The Rocks

The shore is a long way down,
There are many rocks strewn there.
Some are grey and some are brown,
And all are barren and bare.

Strange structures of rock -
So noble, so grand.
What secrets do you lock
In your strange type of land?

So many varieties,
So many shapes.
Some look like deities,
With hoods and capes.

PAUL KLINGER

Green rocks, some black,
Iron ore gives a red.
And when I walk back,
There's a different view instead.

Hard rocks, white crystal, iron ore
Slate, strata, flint and stone.
Is this like the earth's core,
Or is there something unknown?

Tomorrow I go, but you'll still be here.
Humans change like a river,
You won't be affected, you never fear -
Unless an quake makes you quiver.

But there's one thing you can't hide from-
The weather will erode you, just wait and see.
Then you'll know that I can't be wrong
When I tell you that God made you like me.

23. ANIMAL POEMS

I love animals, and I find them amusing. I can easily be inspired to write a poem about an animal. Most of them will be funny poems (I hope).

PAUL KLINGER

The Cat with Three Legs

The cat with three legs and I
Looked at the 'plane in the sky.
She was worried it was a bit low;
I agreed - and said so.

She said "It's a windy day,
So they're using the southern runway.
It really is quite safe
With instrument-landing in place."

I said that she seemed to know
A great deal about how 'planes go.
She said "Yes, when it's foggy
They call on the nearest moggy."

"We stand on the runway
To show the 'planes the way.
With our sparkling cats-eyes,
We guide them down from the skies".

"Unfortunately, on such an occasion
The Control tower used its persuasion
To call on me to stand in
For a pussy who'd hurt her shin".

"But I forgot to move my paw
When the undercarriage hit the floor.
That's why I've only got three,
The fourth deserted me".

"I manage to hobble around
And cover a lot of ground.

Sometimes it's not very nice
When I can't catch any mice."

"I'm always ready to help out
If the airport gives me a shout.
But I'll keep well clear of the wheel,
Two legs - it doesn't appeal."

The Squirrel in the Tree

There's a tree next to our building.
On it a squirrel abides.
I want his input to our meeting
To see what he provides.

He can see our whiteboard clearly
Where it's fixed to the office wall.
He often seems to study it
Whilst nibbling on a windfall.

He knows the technicalities
Behind every single machine.
I turn to ask him to explain
What these equations really mean.

But all he does is fix me
With his little gimlet eyes
And keeps nibbling a nut
From his vantage so high-rise.

Everyone else ignores him
But I know otherwise

He's going to take our data
And sell it to some spies.

There's squirrels around the world
From America to France.
If I were you I'd watch them
'cause their out for the main chance.

London Animals

A Labrador from Lambeth said
To a cat from Camden Town,
"I've been to Golders Green.
Have you been travelling around?".

The cat from Camden referred
To a journey to Saint John's Wood.
"I've miaowed in Maida Vale;
I really don't think _you_ could!".

The dog had barked in Barnet
At a whelk from West Whetstone.
The whelk had to go to Hadley
Where he nearly broke a bone.

A hen from Hendon laid
An egg on the Edgware Road.
She asked were there cocks in Cockfosters,
Or any other nearby abode?

A colt from Colindale said hallo,
As he trotted to Totteridge Green.

He said he'd munched in Muswell Hill-
The nicest place he'd seen.

A duck from Dulwich did quack,
As she waddled to Wandsworth Park,
Followed by a kestrel from Kensington,
Who had to get up with the lark.

An ugly ox from Uxbridge
And a ewe from nearby Yiewsley,
Headed for a haven in Hayes,
Known for its lovely muesli.

A pussy from Purley's in love,
With a moggie from central Morden.
Their neighbour's a womble from Wimbledon
With a brother by the name of Gordon.

The lovely animals of London
Rhyme from Rayners Lane to Ruislip.
But it's standard here in Stanmore
At this point to go for a kip.

The Cat

I know a cat who sits
In a window on the sill,
Observing everything that passes,
Totting up a special bill.

You may think that you can pass
Her window at your ease.

PAUL KLINGER

What you don't think
Is that she's working out the fees.

Kitty has decided
That everyone must pay.
There's no exception
If you pass this way.

The other day a dog
Was barking long and loud,
Probably at the sky
Or maybe at a cloud.

He got charged-
That will be three,
Said kitty; but we don't know
If it's pounds or if it's p.

She doesn't like mice-
They have to pay their dues.
So does anyone else
Who's got a squeak in their shoes.

Kitty cares about pollution.
When the red car down the road
Was making too many fumes
That was against Kitty's code.

That'll be ten
Said Kitty to the car.
Not pence but pounds
Because you drive so far.

And if the postman whistles
A tune she doesn't like,
He'll have to pay up
Next time he's on his bike.

She really doesn't like people
Who make a lot of noise.
It can be anyone,
but normally it's boys.

They all have to pay
It's added to the bill.
You cannot escape
If upset Kitty you will.

Because Kitty wants to retire
To the Isle of Man.
Of cat's without tails
She's really quite a fan.

You can help her pension
For her days by the sea.
Just do something to upset her
And be prepared to pay the fee.

Inkie and I

My lovely friend Inkie, and I
Live on a boat called the Damselfly.
Moored on the canal, by the lake,
Left by the pub is the turning you take.

PAUL KLINGER

We haven't known each other for very long
But I thought I'd sing her a little song,
That's because she's so very sweet-
The nicest person anyone can meet.

Inkie and I get on very well,
But sometimes she tires of me, I can tell.
That's when I decide to leave her be,
And go to live in my house by the tree.

In the morning I come to the boat
And wake her with a sweet little note.
Then she comes out to give me a feed
With a nice tasty bit of bird seed.

Inkie and I, Inkie and I,
We'll be together until we die.
But whereas she'll live for threescore and ten,
I'm afraid I might be done for by then.

24. NONSENSE

The title says it all.

My Bookcase

I've got a green book, a red book, and one covered in black
A yellow book, a white book, and an almanac.
A beige book, a brown book, one coloured maroon.
A blue book, an orange book, and one about the moon.

I've got a thick book, a thin book, one of a square shape,
A big book, a small book, and one covered in tape.
A tall book, a wide book, one that's pocket sized,
One with so many pages, more than you realise.

I've got a Monet book, a Manet book, and one about Rosetti,
A cook book, a recipe book, one about spaghetti.
An Impressionist book, an Expressionist book, one about Dali,
A geology book, a geography book, and one about Bali.

There's a Bronte book, a Galsworthy book:- the Forsyte Saga
A food book, a drinks book - one about lager.
A Christian book, a Catholic book, one about Buddhism;
A Hindu book, a Moslem book, one about Judaism.

A quotations book, a flotations book , and a big encyclopaedia,
A business book, a sports book, and one about the media.
A phone book, address book, one about West End shows
And a book of ex-girlfriends -in case we come to blows.

Sailing on My Gondola

I'm sailing on my gondola
To visit my pagoda
Which is near my pergola
On my island far away.

I'll play my viola
Whilst observing a nebula
Admiring the vista
In the glorious night sky.

By the light of my candelabra
I'll call out "Abracadabra"
And the queen of Sheba
Will appear in the mist.

Was it the Queen of Sheba?
Or maybe it's my mania;
Very possibly I oughta
Go for a lie down.

Then I'll dream of my Alfa
Romeo with its fascia
Which has an added extra
That tells me the time in Spain.

Listening to Santana,
I'll eat a banana
With some added sultana
To give an exotic taste.

I'll play canasta
While travelling to Canberra.

We'll be using algebra
To work out the right route.

Driving around in my Alfa
I'll be quoting from Zarathustra,
Being sustained by pasta
Until the day I die.

Wax in My Ear

I said to the Doctor: I've got wax in my ear!
He said: "You've got an axe up where?"
No Doctor, wax in my ear!
He said "Who's taking Max to the Fair?"

I tried again with a different tack.
I said "Doctor, I have an aural deficiency."
He said "Don't tell me there's fish in the sea."

Doctor, I don't understand what you say.
He said "Nor do I, but that's just my way".

I said "What am I to do about my ear?"
He said "It's a serious thing, a laxative fear."

"But don't worry, we'll get you going in a hurry
I prescribe a spicy hot curry."

I went down to the Indian takeaway.
I said to the man "I want a vindaloo".
He said "A bus to the zoo?"
"Just wait outside for a No. 2,"

ALONE IN THE CITY

I went to the zoo and saw a snake.
I asked him if there was anyone that could cure my ache.

The snake said "What's wrong?"
So I told the serpent: "My ear!"
He said: "You want to see the bear?"
"He's no friend of mine but I'll take you there"

I said to the bear "I have a problem with words"
He said "Why didn't you tell me you love the birds?"
Go to the aviary and there you'll find
Flying creatures of all different kinds".

I went to the aviary and saw a Cockatoo.
I told him I've tried everything, including vindaloo.
The bird said "This is what to do".

There's a place in Africa with a certain tree"
Containing precious oil of didgeridee.
Go there with your dodgy ear.
Go and don't come back here!".

I sailed to Africa in a very big boat.
I couldn't even hear that we were afloat.
But I saw the waves and knew we were at sea
So I went below decks for some tea.

When we landed I sought a camel.
I'd been told it was the best way to travel.

I found a native, he said "There's no camels here.
But I'll give you an elephant to get you there."

But then he thought and said "Where's there?"
I said to the Didgeride tree, "that's where!".

Ah he said with a knowing smile.
"I know why you've come many a mile.
You've got a problem with your ear.
I meet your sort everywhere".

He said "I'll have to charge two dunghill mounds"
I said "Three thousand pounds?"
He said you heard me wrong, it's your ailment.
I'll reiterate the necessary payment.
He said you'll have to pay ten thousand and three
That's English pounds, if you misheard me".

I said "That's cheap at half the price.
I've obviously met someone who's very nice!"

So I travelled on my elephant to the place
The elephant went so slow it was hardly a chase.

When the animal dropped me at the didgeridee tree
There was a small notice nailed to it saying Follow me
So I followed the signs to a small shop
Selling little tubes at ten pounds a shot.

On the tubes it said "To get rid of wax"
I said to the shopkeeper, "Tell me some facts
Does this contain the special oil
Or is it all a cunning foil?"

The shopkeeper told me that the oil was from olive
Which could be got where I live

ALONE IN THE CITY

Not from a native
Or even a relative

He said "You've been taken for a ride
By a trickster from hell!"
I said " I'm so pleased you can confide
That I'll hear as clear as a bell!"

I put in the oil and everything was clear
I even heard a man asking for my fare.

But on the journey back home something strange occurred
My voice got chirpy just like a bird.

My beard felt different, like a feather.
Was it because of a change in the weather?

And when the wind blew I rose in the air
I seemed to be flying with a ruffling of my hair.

I said to a man "Do I look alright?"
He said "Are you asking for a fight?"
I'm not frightened of fighting you
Especially when you look like a cockatoo!"
The next thing I knew, I was back at the zoo.

And there was the bird that had sent me on my trip
I said to him "Thanks a bunch"
He said "Are you offering me lunch?"

"It's your fault I told him that I look like you
Now are you going to tell me what I should do?"

PAUL KLINGER

He said the story has a moral and this is it.
Don't seek advice if you're a bit of a twit.
And if you're a twit who can't hear what's said
If I were you I'd go straight back to bed.

25. SCIENCE FICTION

Only one poem in this section. It was inspired by an ornamental glass pyramid on a colleague's desk.

PAUL KLINGER

The Prism of a Million Colours

Darkness fell over the land
In the middle of the day
The animals were confused;
The people began to pray.

Thunder started to rumble,
Lightning began to flash.
Rain began to fall,
And hailstones to dash

A giant explosion rocked
The buildings in the town
Smoke billowed everywhere
Cloaking houses like a gown.

The gloom persisted for days;
People stayed indoors.
Wondering if this was nature
Or another of their wars.

When the smoke eventually cleared
The people ventured outside
To see what had caused
Them to be so petrified.

There in the ground
Was a massive crater.
Everyone came to look
If not now, later.

Then the ground shook, and light filled the sky.
All the people were scared.

ALONE IN THE CITY

A cloud of dust appeared and something rose-
A wonderful thing appeared.

A giant prism, made of glass
It must have been sixty feet tall.
Light beams danced within it
Bouncing off each glass wall.

The people stared into the glass
Looking to see what was inside.
All of the colours of the rainbow were there,
And many more beside.

Suddenly a beam shot out
Into a field of grass that was near,
Then something amazing happened
To the grass that was growing there.

How many blades of grass in that field?
Possibly many million could be estimated.
Well, each blade had a different colour
To the blade next to where it was situated.

Colours which didn't have a name
Each one unique
Not something science could explain
In Nature it was a freak

But people were fascinated
And stared at the colours in awe.
People came from all around
It was worth a special tour.

Robberies and muggings stopped
Because of this wonderful thing in the town
It had a peaceful effect
And the crime rate went right down.

Very soon the Government realised
They had a very powerful aid
If they could keep this thing
It would be the best decision made.

They didn't know where it came from
Or the reason for its appearance
Meetings at high level were held
With the highest security clearance.

The Prime Minister got on the phone
On a hot line to the States.
One that was used only
For top secret debates.

But there was no need for secrecy
Because in Washington and New York
Giant prisms had appeared
Causing all Americans to talk.

Every American citizen
Had seen a prism somewhere
Because they had appeared
From Boston to Delaware.

It was a similar story in Paris
And other cities in France

ALONE IN THE CITY

This was a deliberate event
Not something happening by chance.

All over the world
Thousands of prisms stood
Each one exactly the same,
But none were understood.

And each one generated
This strange beautiful light
Which generated millions of colours
By day and also by night.

And all the presidents and prime ministers
In lands big and small
Told the same story
The tale was unique, from all.

Peace had fallen upon their land
In the country and the city
Tension and fighting had stopped
Amongst people of each ethnicity.

....

Ten years had passed, time had moved on
But one thing remained the same
Every country had its prism
With each one given a different name.

Some countries had a national holiday;
Treating the prism like a maypole.
Children circled it, flags fluttered
Everyone had a role.

They came to worship this thing
Which had brought eternal calm.
The world was a less stressful place
In which there was no need for alarm.

No country had armies
None had a Navy or an Air force
There was no need for police
All arguments were settled in due course.

A visit to see the colours
Was a vital part of a person's day.
Then all of his or her stresses
Disappeared in a magical way.

So that a special aura
Circled the worldly sphere.
Which was felt across the universe,
Not just inside the stratosphere.

But alas, like so many a tale that's told
A happy ending was not to be had.
I will not tell you the outcome
Whether it was good or it was bad..

But in the early hours
On one clear moonlit night
A man was watching the prism
With its ethereal glowing light.

He saw the beam of light
Bathing the grass all around.

ALONE IN THE CITY

And he saw the beam suddenly turn
Without making any sound.

It focussed on the heavens
It shot out its multi-coloured beam.
The man looked up at the sky
It seemed like a dream.

Others observed the same
All over this world of theirs
The cleverest didn't smile
But dissolved into tears.

Because they realised the time
Had come, the world was now not prepared
No country had any forces
Either alone, or with others shared.

The signal had been sent
There was no turning back
The Earth now was so vulnerable
To an alien attack.

So every person on the planet
To their families, said their goodbyes
And slowly, to the heavens
Lifted up their eyes.

For the good times they had been given
They now had to pay
So mankind, in unison,
Quietly began to pray.

To their God who had looked after them
And been kind to them in His way.
They prayed that their souls
Should return for another day.

THE END

Paul Klinger has been writing poetry for about 15 years, alongside his main hobby, which is art. By profession he is a software quality engineer, and only pursues his hobby when time permits. He lives in North West London.

www.ingramcontent.com/pod-product-compliance
Lightning Source LLC
Chambersburg PA
CBHW060516090426
42735CB00011B/2254